Swimming Through Fire

Swimming Through Fire

Seth Michelson

Press 53
Winston-Salem

Press 53, LLC
PO Box 30314
Winston-Salem, NC 27130

First Edition

A Tom Lombardo Poetry Selection

Copyright © 2017 by Seth Michelson

All rights reserved, including the right of reproduction
in whole or in part in any form except in the case of
brief quotations embodied in critical articles or
reviews. For permission, contact publisher at
editor@Press53.com, or at the address above.

Cover design by Kevin Morgan Watson

Printed on acid-free paper
ISBN 978-1-941209-51-6

for my wife, Vicki, and my sons, Ilan Sebastián and Joaquín

Contents

Introduction	ix
Killers Among Us	3
Terrible Love	4
Papá's War Song	5
Killers Among Us	6
Sloppy Seconds: A Werewolf Manifesto	7
Jesus and Magdelene	8
Happily Evers	9
Killers Among Us	10
Sniper Bullet, Buffalo, NY	11
Elegy XXIV	12
Will We Ever Look Like Doctors?	13
Millennial Haiku	14
Broken Rondeau	15
Killers Among Us	16
Papá's Exhaustion Music	17
Football: A Manifesto	18
Killers Among Us	20
Sexual Violence	21
Strange how we can walk	22
Border Politics	23
Killers Among Us	24
Venceremos	25
Something Like Grace	27
Killers Among Us	28
American Music	29
Terrible Love II	30

For the Beautiful Blond German Woman Sitting Next to Me on a Flight from JFK to LAX	31
Killers Among Us	32
Blindness	33
Cosmopolitical Fugue	34
Killers Among Us	36
Beautiful Black Woman	37
My young son teaches me	39
Killers Among Us	41
Junípero Serra	42
Killers Among Us	44
Acknowlegments	47
Notes	49
Author biography	53

Introduction

There are killers among us. Seth Michelson wants you to know that. He writes poetry to drive that important point into our collective consciousness. Killers surround us and Michelson's poems open our eyes, like broken windows, to the dangers closing in on all of us. Through his deeply figurative poems, we may find a path toward healing for a displaced, disaffected majority of humanity as it swims through the fires of a metaphoric Hell.

These poems range widely in stories: from the Chilean holocaust perpetrated by the fascist dictatorship of General Augusto Pinochet to the assassination of churchgoers in Charleson, South Carolina to the breakup of a marriage; from the holocaust of California's native Indians by St. Junipero Serra to the official sequestration of a proud black soldier to the euthanization of a beloved pet. All of those victims of the killers among us find their way into the penetrating and lovely poetry in Michelson's *Swimming Through Fire*.

There are kakistocratic killers, there are maniacal killers, and then there are killers whom we love and who once loved us. The poem "Broken Rondeau" presents "a story as old as love: his wife / fell from him / to another man." And his life is broken like "a frozen pond" when "someone hurls / a bright red brick / dead-on its center / … cracks racing outward / in sharp fissures / till loud as thunder / splitting the night / it all comes crashing in." Another poem describes the murdered love in a memorable metaphor:

> …consider: how the heart
> can be a sparrow
> struck by a hawk,

leaving behind little
but a burst of feathers
and a fine red mist.

—from "Terrible Love"

How do we prepare our children, the generation that will inherit the killers among us? Perhaps Michelson's advice to his son in "Papa's War Song" is worth considering.

Michelson has read his poems from this collection and his first collection *Eyes Like Broken Windows*, also from Press 53, across the United States, and in Germany, India, Kenya, and Armenia. He's also read in his fluent Spanish in Argentina and in Uruguay, as well as by ambassadorial invitation at the Uruguayan Embassy in Washington, D.C. I am honored to have worked with such a fine poet and to have now selected his second collection for my series.

Tom Lombardo
Press 53 Poetry Series Editor

every demand is a demand of love

—Jean Luc Nancy

the testimony of love as the practice of freedom

—bell hooks

Swimming Through Fire

Killers Among Us

Somewhere a war ends.
No joy.
Only weeping.

Terrible Love

If my wife could lop
my hands off, dry them
to a reddish jerky,
she would,
setting them palm-up
on her desk
as macabre candy dishes,
that she'd pile high
with bright-colored
jelly beans: a fallen
rainbow of sweetness,
a warning to any passer-by
pausing to snack,
consider: how the heart
can be a sparrow
struck by a hawk,
leaving behind little
but a burst of feathers
and a fine red mist.

Papá's War Song

for my son, Joaquín

Joaquín: bright blue starlight
traveled centuries
to sing from your eyes,
born in the flooded junction
of the Río de la Plata
and the Los Angeles River,
mestizo: part gaucho,
part L.A. Dodger, red hair,
dulce de leche skin, a Latin
heartbeat: pum-PUM.
So please hear me, Quinito,
when I say look both ways in life
then look some more,
because the local mobs,
O they will come:
chanting beneath burning pitchforks,
and they'll forgive nothing
as they strike
to take it all from you, mi Quinito,
against which your best chance
is a quick song
and a hard right hook.

Killers Among Us

Where to sing when home
is your gas-soaked skin,
and everyone around you
a struck match?

Sloppy Seconds: A Werewolf Manifesto

"It's so hard to work on Wall Street,"
the werewolf whines to his wife
over a glass of chilled Chablis
in their Tribeca kitchen.
She nods, coos "Another
oven-roasted pig ear?
Toasted with brown sugar,
just the way you like them."
But alone, lost in thought,
he snarls to the winds
till his wife grasps her duty,
drops softly to her knees.
She unzips him and soon sweat
is rising through his back fur,
pork-breath filling the room
as his panted rage
singes her ears: She hears
an oil derrick pounding dry earth—
flash of tooth, roar of spleen—
and rips out his songless throat.

Jesus and Magdalene

> "Christ loved her more than all the other disciples
> and used to kiss her often on the mouth."
> —*Gospel of Philip,* Logion 55:3-4

In an acolyte's empty home
in the seaside town of Galilee,
I lie down alone
on a straw mat to rest.
Why when I've converted
water to wine, the blind to seeing,
are you all I think of: *Sweet*
Magdalene, companion, sinner.
How your voice broke a dam
when today I refused you
more than a kiss,
but what I withheld
will become your blessing
by denial. Yet all I see
are your curves: firm calves, hips, lips,
the late sunlight like honey
drizzled across your cleavage,
and soon I'm whispering *Sweet*
Magdalene, singing
the body in its loneliness,
this consecration of being,
the resurrection of my fist.

Happily Evers

Somewhere a groom slips
his hubby from a tux.
How else to sing of love?

Killers Among Us

Somewhere a judge
gives a teen life in prison.
A door bangs closed
on both.

Sniper Bullet, Buffalo NY
> 23 October 1998, 10 p.m.

A window shatters, then his spine
bursts into splinters
before the bullet, molten orange,
clips his aorta, exits his chest.
As that bullet, baptized
by blood, goes whistling off
into night sky, how
Doctor Barnett Slepian,
like the glass he's rinsing, falls
and shatters on the kitchen floor:
a father splayed out, dying
on terra cotta tile
beside his teen son, who, shocked,
stands staring, staring:
through the hole
in the broken window
where early snowfall drifts in,
the first flakes of a winter
so dark, so cold.

Elegy XXIV

Another dinner: cold
spaghetti and meatballs,
and your empty chair.

Will We Ever Look Like Doctors?

Baby-faced at forty-two, she hits
Exam Room Six with brutal news:
the burly mechanic
wringing greasy fingers
has stage-four sarcoma: *That lump
in your throat, Sir, it can kill you.*
She stops speaking, flips
closed the chart, looks over
red reading glasses
into his confusion: twin
avalanches in his eyes,
and she knows he's thinking,
What isn't falling away?
So she points to an x-ray:
explains cloud-like shapes
that make his left cheek twitch
the way a small bird shivers
in a gust of chilly wind
or the way a street
shudders in an earthquake
before buckling inward.
How are you feeling?, she asks,
laying a hand on his knee.
Not now, Sweetie, he grunts.
Just send the doc in.

Millennial Haiku

My five-year-old asks,
"Dad, do we have a rocket?
I'd like to see space."

Broken Rondeau

It's a story old as love: his wife
fell from him
to another man. This
she told him, weeping;
what to do when there's no wisdom?
When the heart shrivels
like a plastic doll
tossed into flame? Forms
break, young man;
lives get broken.
How the mind
is a frozen pond
in the silence of winter
when someone hurls
a bright red brick
dead-on into its center:
the origin of hurt,
cracks racing outward
in sharp fissures
till loud as thunder
splitting the night,
it all comes crashing in.

Killers Among Us

Somewhere a newborn
wiggles in a dumpster.
How now to sing
community?

Papá's Exhaustion Music

Again: I said no!
But behind me in the back seat,
my young sons keep fighting,
our cramped Hyundai
a toddler battlefield: smoke
billowing up between them, heel-kicks
flashing across my rearview
as we speed to market, to market,
to buy a fat bottle of gin,
a late addition to the list of eggs,
string cheese, carrots, milk.
So let me, sheesh!, O pretty please
begin again: I said no!
I said Stop it, boys.
I said Zip it.
I said ¡Ya, basta, chicos!
I said Striving to win in life
is a Sisyphean myth.
I said Dwell in the scent of the rose,
high above the thorns.
Yet on they brawl, these
tiny hooligans.
How to make it cease?
Drop the Law on them
the way God
tablet-smashed Moses?
Lead them to the language
lighting the flowers
that dream of being
so much more to the world
than too much gin?

Football: A Manifesto

Of course in a game like this
of bone-cracking collisions, the brain,
too, would be perturbed: yellow
Jello shaken in a lidded bowl
till it turns to watery soup. So it is
these headlong warriors
are a lot like childhood you: true
believers, born again
and again by forgetting:
memory-loss their signature
in disappearing ink
of lives concussed, skull-drubbed.
Punch-drunk comes to mind, a brain
befogged by chronic violence,
the blows in football
more boom of wrecking ball
than tangle of playful bodies.
So these men believe
in a mouthpiece
as extra padding for nonstop wallopings,
and 64% of us believe, too,
this is the apex of entertainment:
eleven men in shiny red
and eleven more in dull silver
lining up for the QB's signal
to scramble brains, turning
water to wine for team owners
who on TV after the Big One
slap the backs of their bruised galoots,
who, brain-mashed, cheer, too,

spritzing the room with champagne
as they babble to reporters
about hard work, team chemistry,
"I thank God, who blessed me,"
He who loved them so much
He created them as meat.

Killers Among Us

Somewhere in a bar
a man drugs a woman's drink.
How now to sing
of libido?

Sexual Violence

Watch my teen niece, vegan, snap
the leg off a roasted chicken
and you'll get it: how easily
the body is unmade. It's the carving plate,
to dinner, a hungry family set to feast:
on thigh, breast, and wing
of decapitated creature.
Whose mind, the philosopher asked,
is inconsequential in its absence?
Not my niece's, stalked
by thoughts of home invasion:
late at night, alone, in bed half-
dreaming, when she wakes
to a window shattered, footfall
nearing her room, where
she squints into outer darkness
and sees nothing but her own fear,
till he's on her: growling
hot into her ear, his stench
all sweat and sperm and beer,
pinning her at knife-point to her sheet—
how horrifying the eaters' smiles
at the plate of skinned meat, broken bones.

Strange how we can walk

    into new light each morning, same
    city, same sidewalk, but somehow
    this daybreak: downtown L.A., late May,
    and you're walking alone,
    a white flame, the birds singing
    as they mull yesterday's news:
    aortic stenosis; *Your heart, Sir, it's*
    leaking. So you become
    in this morning's light
    a blanked-out human figure, edges
    rippling with heat: a star
    bleeding luminosity into a dark universe,
    causing you to cry out in a voice
    that's both yours and isn't
    How much bludgeoning—
    by joy, by cruelty—
    as we're unmade by living?

Border Politics

Brisenia Flores and her father, Raúl,
were shot to death in Arizona, killed
by locals who stalked the border
the way eels slither a river.
Arizona is O'odham, the region's
oldest known language, and means
"small spring," though the killers' interests
didn't include etymologies.
Instead they patrolled the small spring
with GPS, smartphones, and pistols
to convolute the ancient story
of human migration. To guard
their turf, these Minutemen
vanished Brisenia and Raúl
in a few, booming trigger-pulls,
and vanished, too, another lungful
of hope from the human family,
hurt like seabirds caught
in a tanker's angry spill: oil
in their eyes and ears, oil
burning their throats as they tip
and paddle in blind circles,
unable to see: how
they're each crying,
and how they're also each
somehow a clear, small spring.

Killers Among Us

      for Junebug, euthanized 4/23/11

Somewhere an old Beagle
offers a paw to the vet.
O noose of obedience,
neck-snap of fealty!

Venceremos

for Víctor Jara

They snapped
your fingers, one
by one, pain
exploding
from each knuckle,
till agony, only
the agony
of your hand
was real and present.
Everything else
was echo: of bone
snapped
and crooked
fingers: pain
of snakes
set on fire,
of moths
stitched alive
into a collector's book,
and you
pinned there,
Víctor Jara,
writhing
in bloody dirt,
one more body
amidst the many
being kicked,
slapped and cursed:
in Estadio Chile,
O civic cathedral,

pit of erasures
where the Comandante
bent over you
and hissed
into your ear, *Víctor,*
you'll never again
strum or sing,
at least not
in this world, traitor.

Something Like Grace

My youngest son, part boy, part comet,
turns five today, life of orbit,
of flaming cartwheels through night sky,
of tumbling galaxies of possibility,
while a few hours south of here
someone else's son
sits chained to a metal table: two
detectives asking him why,
at twenty-one, he shot up a church,
killed nine book-loving truth-seekers?
Bless their innocence, and bless my boy,
so new to this soot-stained world,
voice of water, breath of pine
stirred by the gentlest wind,
his mind the starlight that fills these hills
we're riding through
to reach his birthday party,
our windows open as our hearts,
Los Intoxicados blaring from the radio,
Nunca quise tanto a nadie como vos,
and his My Little Pony cake
tucked snug on the seat beside me,
buckled in, safe in its dream
of pink ponies grazing sweet creation
beneath a protective, plastic dome
as we whip through turns
and split the night
singing out full-throated.

Killers Among Us

Somewhere a cop
tackles a violent teen.
O the ways we meet,
O the singing night rain!

American Music

> for Mark Matthews, 1894-2005

In the 1890s, still a child, Mark
delivered newspapers by pony.
At 15 he saw Buffalo Soldiers, fell
in love: became one. This
is the story of a boy turned pony
turned buffalo turned starry music.
It's the news of marksmanship,
of gall and grit,
of gargantuan human spirit: Mark
who alone tracked down Pancho Villa
deep in Mexico and released him,
believing no one should be stalked,
shackled, and shipped like goods. Yes,
Mark knew. He escorted King George
to FDR's White House for fish chowder.
Mark, a warrior with a cellist's heart.
Mark playing "Taps" by bugle
at Arlington funerals,
though always hidden in the woods:
nothing but that same, sad tune
drifting down from a clutch of trees
to wash over the huddled mourners
like an otherworldly breeze. Listen
carefully to the wind today
and you'll hear him
still playing.

Terrible Love II

She wants my body
in pieces: head
floating in a jar
of pinkish water
on her kitchen windowsill
beside cilantro, basil, sage,
my skull a trophy: mouth
taut, finally silent,
face frozen in fear,
staring out, blinkless,
at what we once were:
a town walloped
by colliding hurricanes:
wind and thunder
and thrashing rain,
the screech of metal
bending
till buildings splintered.

For the Beautiful Blond German Woman Sitting Next to Me on a Flight from JFK to LAX

Because you spilled your plastic cup
of Perrier across my lap, drenching
my jeans, I want to use my tongue
to trace the word *Seide*
up and down you till you shiver.
Who doesn't love a blond aristocrat
in white jeans, a lemony blouse,
a trail of strawberry freckles
plunging down her cleavage
and ending where?
And I'm sorry for your kin
with names like *Schutzstaffel*, *Reichsführer*,
men who struggled to dream
and goose-stepped through life
like humorless children.
And I'm sorry, too, for wanting
to lick you open in all your sugary shiksaness.
I'd never do it. We Jews
don't eat *Schweineschnitzel* or *Rippenbraten*,
especially not when ecstatically married
to the rebel Eve of God's wet dreams.
But this in-flight crossword puzzle
on which I'm doodling
is themed "Getting Around."

Killers Among Us

Somewhere a dad tsks
his teen daughter's skirt.
Hurt and more hurt,
the drifting.

Blindness

Saramago was blind, or his characters were,
to the invisibility of justice, the way
a living hand, so warm and capable,
braces your shoulder when the subway
jerks: How everyone stumbles,
a jumbled mash of staggered
strangers, sheepish thank yous,
the air bright with sudden kindness,
a common tenderness revealed.
It buzzes through the wagons
as they resume their screechy pull:
for the next station, platforms
yet unseen, but surely out there,
soon to take form the way clouds
out of nowhere appear,
cohering sudden beauty,
and how Saramago, or at least his
characters, can't trust in emergence,
not without seeing it first-hand,
so they beat their heads with rocks
till their foreheads bleed
and they gouge at their eyes
with their own fingers
till all they see is white pain: lives
auto-erased: the invisible world
stripped of hope, possibility,
so they throw themselves
naked into icy lakes, pitch themselves
headlong off seaside cliffs,
desperate to find and feel
all that's unfelt, unseen.

Cosmopolitical Fugue

Syrian immigrants smash on the rocks
off Lesbos where Sappho sang *Don't shatter
my heart with fierce pain*, the line
looping in my head as I wake from eye surgery:
the soft white of my right globe
sliced open, leaking: the recovery room
blurred red as I struggle to resurface
from dark waters, listening to radio news:
a Mexican immigrant is speaking Spanish
from an apple orchard in Pennsylvania:
a mí me gusta la vida, hustle to pick: ten
hours per day, six days a week, don't even stop
to pee, *es mi vida*, O glossy fruit,
harvest of dreams; take a break, dear reader,
to lift an apple skyward till it gleams:
juicy ruby, snug and certain
in the world of your grip, what was once
the picker's now yours: sweetness
torn into being, stacked and sold
by farmers in flannel shirts, muddy boots,
who flip basketfuls onto roadside tables,
apples spilling out like immigrants
from dinghies flipped by rough surf,
eyes stung by spindrift, two bodies
already swallowed by the salty roil,
the rest slapping at its icy surface
in smashed hope as they cry out:
the pain of shattered migration,
hope a splintered dinghy,
and the Mexican immigrant just now saying

lo que te llevas contigo
es solamente lo necesario,
his voice so clear I see him here:
picking apples from my IV stand
and tossing each burning orb
to a wicker basket across the room: fruit
slashing through the space between us,
red trails of celestial vapor,
red as the surgeon's first cut, our vision
flooded with seeing,
so pick an apple, famished reader,
and crush it between your teeth: its juice
our prayer filling your mouth,
an invitation to hope.

Killers Among Us

A rusted gate
gives itself to wind,
bangs and bangs
in an empty field.

Beautiful Black Woman
for my dear friend Dunia

When it finally came, delayed
for decades like a memoir
promising taboo truths, yes, when
finally it came, how, O my lord,
it broke you open like a scream:
that shatters a full wine glass,
juice flooding the table, the room
bright with the dizzying scent
of rich, dark fruit: you released, Dunia,
finally hearing "You're a beautiful black woman,"
yes, biracial you, Dunia,
so much more than most of us
can dream of being: a self
of convergent rivers, hidden currents,
glittering surface: yes, you, Dunia,
who'd been teased for years:
as dirty white, stained, or as too white
to be a Panther's proud daughter,
though of course you are: remember
how we often shun
the best humans, make of them
pariahs or loons, think Francis of Assisi:
how he dwelled in love for all creatures
and so was mocked, scorned, and beaten
the way bullies will target
the gentle-hearted bookworm,
and how you, Dunia, were trained
to think yourself constant intruder: no
group, no home, a mutt kicked
through every gutter, so when finally

it came, those three blessed words,
beautiful black woman, it was love
in language, recognition in lightning,
a honey-voiced welcoming into truth:
your heart bursting into light
for us all to bask in, and how,
even better, you finally heard the music
of your own symphonic, shining skin.

My young son teaches me

how we love disorder when he
flips the trashcan in the kitchen: sticky

soup cans, damp cardboard
everywhere. What was once

discarded is now reborn: right
here, on cold white tile. And

when I drop to my knees
beside my son, deep in it,

how he teaches me: to be
typhoon jubilant, to smile

all peach-cobbler, eyes
twin lakes of fire, as he squeals

the felicity of beasts, kicking
his feet with spastic pleasure,

his tiny fingers raking my face,
which disappears: a break

in space-time, where we hover,

no pain, no grief:
only me gone gooftoothy,

and my son all squirms
and pink giggles as not two

not one body tumbles,
joy-drenched, hooting.

Killers Among Us

Looking up, see the lie:
the white moon
is bloodshot, mute.

Junípero Serra

A rusty chain of slave camps rattles
from San Francisco to San Diego,
kicking up dust, ghosts of *indios*
stirred and set again to work:
laying adobe brick upon brick
into colonial missions, whitewashed
visions glimmering pink with sunset.
Copper bells peal vespers,
and *indios*, too, sing the wane of day
or they're stripped and whipped
till their flesh shines its fury
the way Christ wept tears of blood,
and you, Junípero Serra,
so far from Mallorca,
from *buñuelos* baked hot
in Spanish ovens by Moriscos: those
proto-*indios*, Catholics by blade,
abandoned by frightened angels
who took flight with wings in flames
when Spanish tourists said
Burn the locals. Yes,
you're a saint now, Junípero: a name
churchmarms teach their students:
Be Juníperos, my children,
reap what God has sown for us
in this fecund valley, O Alta California,
O Junípero, know we see you:

enthroned after a meal
of roasted corn, wine, and pigeon,
the black rope of your holy belt
loosened as you belch and grin,
picking at your yellowed teeth
with a sucked-bare wing bone.

Killers Among Us

The wars end,
not the hatred.
How to sing
of futures?

Acknowledgments

With gratitude for the diligent effort of the many underappreciated and exhausted poetry editors, as well as their many generous screening readers and their public readership, the poet wishes to thank the following poetry anthologies and literary journals for their relentless advocacy of the importance of the literary arts, including their publication of his work: *Bellevue Literary Review*, *The Colorado Review*, *Hip Mama*, *MAYDAY Magazine*, *Michigan Quarterly Review*, *Moonday*, *Nadwah* (Egypt), *The New Humanist* (United Kingdom), *Poems with Heart*, *Red Sky: Poetry on the Global Epidemic of Violence against Women*, *RiversEdge: A Journal of Art and Literature*, *Poetry in the Windows*, *Poetry International*, *Six Seasons* (India), *Split This Rock*, *TAB: A Journal of Poetry and Poetics*, *Terminus*, and *Variant Vibrancies* (India).

Crucially, too, the poet wishes to thank Kevin Morgan Watson, the visionary founder of Press 53, and Tom Lombardo, its inimitable poetry editor. In many ways this book is more theirs than the poet's. They are bulwarks against the surging tide of icy, dark waters.

A deep, deferential bow is due, too, to the many poets and writers who through no fault of their own have directly and sometimes unknowingly inspired and supported this book, namely

Thomas Lux, Alicia Partnoy, Rodger LeGrand, Marjorie Agosín, Jimmy Santiago Baca, Stephen Dobyns, Tamara Kamenszain, Roberto Ignacio Díaz, David Lloyd, Robert Masterson, Zulema Moret, Sappho, Rati Saxena, Amir Or, Sesshu Foster, Alberto Moreiras, Antonio Reyes, Dante, Pär Hannson, Martin Glaz Serup, Nezahualcoyotl, Ricardo Dominguez, Gunnar Wærness, David St. John, Carol Muske Dukes, Mark Irwin, Marco Fajardo, Virgil, Joan Larkin, Marie Howe, Allen Grossman, Greg Williamson, Natasha Sajé, Daniel Dugas, Rachel Simon, Homer, Ross Gay, Pat Rosal, Alexandra Soiseth, Zbigniew Herbert, Pat Dunn, Ko Un, Victoria Estol, Melisa Machado, Johannes Gorannson, Natalia Romero, Tomas Tranströmer, Ellen Mayock, Deborah Miranda, Christopher Okigbo, Lesley Wheeler, Leah Green, Alston Cobourn, Suzanne Keen, Genevieve Kaplan, Sean Bernard, Jessica Piazza, Simon Ortiz, Gail Wronsky, Emily Dickinson, Jesse Lee Kercheval, Juan Gelman, Chuck Rosenthal, and Steve McCormick.

R.I.P. Cody Todd (1978-2016).

Notes

"Papá's War Song"

A *gaucho* is an Argentine cowboy. They are metonyms for a certain set of conceptions of *argentinidad*, or Argentine identity, and as such they function as cornerstones of the founding mythos of the modern Argentine state.

The Río de la Plata is a river and estuary empty-ing into the Atlantic Ocean. It conjoins the Paraná and Uruguay rivers, tracing a fluid border between Argentina and Uruguay and serving as a longstanding, major waterway for global trade.

Dulce de leche is a very popular sweet in Argentina and beyond. It has a taste, texture, and color somewhat similar to creamy caramel.

Pum-pum is the Spanish-language equivalent of the English-language "lub-dub," meaning the onomatopoeic descriptor of the sound of a human heartbeat.

Quinito is the affectionate nickname for my young son, Joaquín. It is formed by adding the diminutive suffix "–ito" to the common nickname for the name Joaquín, which is Quino.

"Sniper Bullet, Buffalo, NY"

Barnett Abba Slepian II (1946-1998), an obstetrician-gynecologist, was shot to death through his kitchen window on 23 October 1998 by an anti-choice terrorist hiding outside. At the time of his murder, Dr. Slepian was warming soup for dinner for his wife and four sons after attending a memorial service for his deceased father. The bullet that murdered Dr. Slepian narrowly missed his wife and two of his sons. The terrorist, James Charles Kopp, was tried and convicted of second-degree murder, and he is currently serving a prison sentence of twenty-five years to life.

"Venceremos"

The title of the poem "Venceremos" is the first person plural present indicative form of the infinitive verb *vencer*, meaning to win, triumph, defeat, overcome, or vanquish. In the context of the poem, the title of the poem could therefore be roughly translated as "We shall triumph" or "We shall overcome."

Víctor Lidio Jara Martínez (1932-1973) was a popular Chilean singer-songwriter, teacher, human-rights activist, and theater director. He was a leading voice in the *Nueva Canción* movement, blending folk music with socially conscious lyrics. This was likely the reason for his abduction on 12 September 1973 by the fascist dictatorship of General Augusto Pinochet, which resulted in his torture and ultimately his murder on or about 15 September 1973 in Estadio Chile in Santiago, Chile.

"Border Politics"

On 30 May 2009 at around 1a.m. in Arivaca, Arizona, Brisenia Ylianna Flores (9) and her father, Raul Flores, Jr., (29) were shot to death during a home invasion led by the aspiring leader of a burgeoning militant nationalist, isolationist group calling itself the Minutemen American Defense. During the home invasion, Brisenia's mother, Gina Gonzalez (31), was shot three times but survived by playing dead. According to Gina's testimony in court during the trial of one of the accused assailants, Brisenia was shot to death at point-blank range while pleading for her life. The three perpetrators of the crime were Shawna Forde (1967-), Jason Eugene Bush (1974-), and Albert Gaxiola (1967-), and each was convicted of murder, with Forde and Bush being sentenced to death and Gaxiola being sentenced to life imprisonment without parole plus fifty-four years.

"Something Like Grace"

On 17 June 2015, Dylann Roof (1994-) shot to death nine people and wounded a tenth in the Emanuel Africa Methodist Episcopal Church in Charleston, South Carolina, with the aim of inciting a race war in the United States. The nine murder victims were Cynthia Marie Graham Hurd, 54; Susie Jackson, 87; Ethel Lee Lance, 70; Depayne Middleton-Doctor, 49; Clementa Carlos Pinckney, 41; Tywanza Sanders,

26; Daniel Simmons, 74; Sharonda Coleman-Singleton, 45; and Myra Thompson, 59.

"Blindness"

José Saramago (1922-2010) was an acclaimed Portuguese author whose literary distinctions include the 1998 Nobel Prize for Literature. This poem responds to his novels in general, with specific links to *Ensaio sobre a Cegueira* (1995; *Blindness*, 1997).

"Junípero Serra"

Junípero Serra (1713-1784) was a Roman Catholic priest and founder of nine missions stretching from San Diego, California, to San Francisco, California, as well as five missions in Querétaro, México. For his work he was canonized by Pope Francis in 2015 and is known as the Apostle of California. Of note that system of colonization propelled the genocide of nearly 300,000 Native Americans in the region.

Seth Michelson is an award-winning poet, professor, and translator whose collections of poetry include *Swimming Through Fire*, *Eyes Like Broken Windows*, and the chapbooks *House in a Hurricane*, *Kaddish for My Unborn Son*, and *Maestro of Brutal Splendor*. His translations of poetry include the books *The Ghetto* (Tamara Kamenszain, Argentina), *roly poly* (Victoria Estol, Uruguay), *Poems from the Disaster* (Zulema Moret, Argentina/Spain), *Red Song* (Melisa Machado, Uruguay), and *Dreaming in Another Land* (Rati Saxena, India). He currently teaches the poetry of the Americas at Washington and Lee University, as well as in a high-security prison for undocumented, unaccompanied youth. He welcomes contact through his website, sethmichelson.com

CPSIA information can be obtained
at www.ICGtesting.com
Printed in the USA
LVHW042059141220
674147LV00009B/1945